D0499895

# BRITNEY SPEARS

## The Biography of Britney Spears

## University Press

# CONTENTS

# PROLOGUE

"**M**s. Spears, I'm afraid we have to pass."

The middle-aged man on the other side of the desk wasn't even looking at her. He was looking at her mother, as though it was Lynne who had handed over the demo, Lynne who had spent the last month rehearsing like crazy, Lynne who had been living with butterflies in her stomach ever since hearing that she had a time slot blocked out at the recording studio. All the excitement, the thrill, the drive of the past few weeks seemed to fade into nothingness.

Strike three.

There wasn't much else to say. She could try her best to convince him otherwise, but what good would that do now? Besides, though she was not usually shy, her voice seemed to be trapped in her throat. She balled her hands into fists in her lap and let her mother speak for her.

"I see. Well. Thank you for your consideration."

"Sure." The executive nodded without any particular interest. His eyes darted sideways, a bare glance at the fifteen-year-old girl in the other chair. Then his gaze slid on, returning to the stack of papers on his desk. She eyed the demo tape where it sat on the corner, part of a stack of others. Should they ask for it back? He ought to just give it back anyway.

But it was too late now. Her mother was standing, sliding a hand through the crook of her arm, guiding her out of the office. They were quiet as they left. It wasn't until they were in the elevator that she burst out, "He didn't sound sorry."

"That's how it goes sometimes, Britney. He's a busy man."

"But the tape was special. Mr. Rudolph said so."

"Of course it was, honey. But it was just – wasn't for him. That's all."

By the time the elevator reached the lobby, Britney was caught somewhere between screaming and crying. All day they'd spent here in New York, traipsing around, handing her demo out to the record labels recommended by Mr. Rudolph. She had expected that a man like Mr. Rudolph would know exactly where she should go to be welcomed with open arms. She had a talent; she knew she did. It wasn't as though this was her first rodeo, anyhow…

"There's still Jive Records," her mother reminded her. "We haven't heard back from them yet."

Britney sighed.

"Maybe I should just call Mr. Pearlman," she said. "Tell him that I'll join Innosense after all."

"If that's what you want."

Britney stopped in the middle of the city street to think about it. Was that what she wanted? When Lou Pearlman had called her father and asked to speak to her about joining the girl group he was putting together, it had sounded like the next logical step – the next big thing. But then her mother had called their friend Larry Rudolph, and asked him what he thought about it, and Mr. Rudolph had sent Britney to record the demo, recommending that she go solo – now that she had the idea in her mind, could she let go of it? She believed in herself, in her voice, in her drive – she believed in the music…

What she didn't want was to go back to Kentwood, Louisiana, to her old life and her school and her boyfriend and her basketball team. She had more in her, she just knew it; she was ready to take on the world.

If only the world would cooperate!

Her mother put an arm around her and shepherded her towards the parking garage.

"Come on, honey. It's been a long day."

A long day, with visits to four record labels – and three rejections. From the fourth, Jive Records, she had heard nothing at all.

Britney had heard that no news was good news. But at the moment, she would have given anything for her mother's cell phone to ring. She would have given anything to hear. *Good news, Ms. Spears, we'd like to sign Britney to a five-year contract...*

But all she heard was the hustle and bustle of New York City, moving on without her.

Britney heaved another sigh – and then straightened herself up. This wasn't it, she promised herself. She was too determined, and she'd come too far already. So what if three out of four labels had rejected her demo? Her mother was right – there was still Jive.

And after that, she'd find someone else to sing to.

She had to remember to believe in herself, in her voice, in the music. She had to give herself a chance...

...one more time.

# CHAPTER ONE

**A** sign outside the local high school in Kentwood, Louisiana, read Drive carefully, live prayerfully. It was a bare-bones basic sum-up of the close-knit, God-fearing, church-going community, but an accurate one all the same.

The Spears family fit in like a round peg in a circular hole. James Parnell Spears – Jamie, to everyone who knew him – was the patriarch. He owned a successful construction company and was also involved in business development. His wife Lynne was a diminutive, sweet, quiet-voiced woman; the pair had married in 1976, and though their marriage was not without its ups and downs, in the end they always seemed to come back to each other.

In the early eighties, the Spears family enjoyed a rather traditional lifestyle; busy, to be sure, but normal. Jamie oversaw his crew, Lynne ran a small daycare center, and their children got the benefit of two parents who undeniably loved each other and were happy to pour their attentions into their progeny. Their oldest, Bryan, was born in 1977. The first of the girls, Britney Jean, was born a handful of years later in 1981; the third and final Spears child was born in 1991, leading to a ten-year age gap between herself and her older sister. Functionally, for the first ten years of her life, Britney was the youngest child, and her bright, happy-go-lucky personality reflected that role to a tee.

From the time she could walk – and, more importantly, talk – Britney was eagerly singing, dancing, and generally entertaining her family. By age three, she had eagerly convinced her parents to enroll her in dance lessons there in Kentwood; her enthusiasm for movement and her natural sense of rhythm led to her being chosen for a solo spot in the annual show. It wasn't just dancing and movement that attracted her attention, though; she was eager to share her voice, and had a good grasp of tone, projection, and key even from her youngest years. "She was always singing," her mother Lynne recalled fondly years later. "She would never hush."

Other vivid memories were of a two-year-old Britney taking over the bathroom, standing in front of the vanity mirror, and singing her heart out, using a hairbrush as a microphone.

Britney found early inspiration in the popular singers of her childhood, often heard on the radio and seen in music videos on TV. Years later, she would look back on her early days spent listening to Madonna, Janet Jackson, and Whitney Houston, thinking of them as major influences not only on her singing style but on her desire to sing at all. They were her three favorite artists, special among the many that she listened to at the time and since; she recalls singing along to them "day and night in my living room." Another major influence was Mariah Carey, who was "one of the main reasons I started singing." Her older brother Bryan recalled Britney's early performances too, all too well; remembering his little sister dancing and singing along to Madonna's *Like a Prayer* in the family room, he said wryly, "It was very annoying."

When Britney was five years old, she made her first official stage debut, singing *What Child is This* at her own kindergarten graduation.

The Spears family, like many in the Bible Belt area in which they lived, were devout church-goers. Britney was raised to be God-fearing and a regular attendee at the local Southern Baptist church in town. Along with the opportunity to learn about her family's religious beliefs, going to church gave Britney yet another outlet for her growing vocal skill; she loved singing the hymns, and her enthusiastic voice was clearly audible among the rest of the congregation.

Britney was always delighted when given a chance to perform – which usually happened anytime that her mother welcomed a visitor, whether it be a new neighbor or someone who popped in just about every day, like Lynne's older sister Sandra.

Britney was one of the lucky few born not only with talent, but the ability to realize it at a very young age. "I was in my own world," she later said of what it was like to be singing practically from the moment she emerged from the womb. "I found out what I'm supposed to do at an early age."

But it wasn't just the talent that did it for Britney; it was also her motivation. Talent isn't enough to launch a career; drive, on the other hand, can make a five-year-old convince her family that she's going to be a star. Britney was even more fortunate in being born with both.

# CHAPTER TWO

J amie and Lynne might have expected their daughter to lose some of her hyper-focus on performing as she started school; if they did, they were convinced otherwise very quickly.

Britney attended elementary school there in Kentwood. She was a decent student, but academia was far from her priorities list, which included singing, dancing, gymnastics, and proving to the world that she could do anything she set her mind to. Shortly after beginning dance and voice lessons, she started to compete in talent competitions; by the time she was six, she'd won the first of what would prove to be many, including both local and state shows.

Her interest in gymnastics corresponded nicely with her fascination with dance and movement overall. On the small side for her age, Britney was slim and petite, and the gymnastics training helped her to build up the endurance that would allow her to use her energies to the max.

Britney was still fascinated by music videos and other music-driven programs on television. In 1989, at seven years old, she caught the first episode of the reboot of the Mickey Mouse Club on the Disney Channel. A variety show in which young performers were showcased for dancing and singing. She had stars in her eyes just thinking of it! Thus, she began a campaign to convince her parents that she belonged on the show.

Years later, Britney would explain how seeing other kids her age appear on television had motivated her. "When people see things on TV that they can't do, that should make them want to go out there and make something of themselves. That's how I looked at it."

There was no denying that Britney's enthusiasm for performing would fit in well with the other kids on the Mickey Mouse Club. She could sing the theme song perfectly on key – and at top volume. *M-I-C! K-E-Y! M-O-U-S-E!* But Jamie and Lynne were still a little hesitant; Britney was a few years younger than any of the other kids, too.

It was the problem of her age that led to her being turned down when she finally convinced her mother to take her to Atlanta, Georgia, to audition for the show. Britney was only eight at the time, and the casting director, Matt Casella, agreed with Lynne that Britney was a little too young. Still, in her audition, it was clear that she had the talent and focus of a teenager – almost that of an adult. Casella suggested that Lynne consider taking Britney elsewhere to allow her another outlet for her developing voice. He introduced Britney and her mother to a talent agent.

Nancy Carson was an agent based out of New York City. Like Casella, she was impressed with Britney's skill – and her determination. After observing her demonstrate her vocal and dance talents, Carson told Lynne that Britney had what it took – but she still needed some training. A handful of local classes in voice, dance, and gymnastics weren't quite enough to give Britney the edge she needed; Carson suggested that Britney be enrolled in a performing arts school, namely the Professional Performing Arts School in New York.

From Kentwood, Louisiana, New York City seemed an almost impossible distance. Commuting was out of the question; nothing short of a big move would make the school a possibility for Britney. Lynne was still doubtful; Jamie Spears, on the other hand, was optimistic. It wasn't just a case of doting parents thinking too much of their daughter. Now, they had both a casting director and a talent agent urging them to provide more training to Britney. If the eight-year-old hadn't shown promise, surely they would have said as much!

Not long after, the Spears family broke in half for

a time, with Jamie and Bryan staying at home in Kentwood, and Lynne taking Britney and her newborn baby sister to live in a small apartment in New York.

The Professional Performing Arts School, or PPAS, was brand-new when Britney enrolled, having been founded in 1990. It was set up to provide education to aspiring members of the performing arts, especially to youths who were actively pursuing a career in the arts even while they were attending middle and high school. Located in the Hell's Kitchen district of Manhattan, the school would come to boast an impressive roster of alumni, including actress Claire Danes, singer Alicia Keyes, actor Jesse Eisenberg – and Britney Spears.

While throwing herself into her new educational environment and making the most of the new avenues of training she was exposed to, Britney was determined that the move to New York wouldn't solely be about attending PPAS. With her mother and baby sister accompanying her to every casting call she could find, she landed her first professional role as an understudy for the lead role in an off-Broadway musical, *Ruthless!* The lead was played by Laura Bell Bundy; Britney shared her duties as an understudy with another budding actress about her age, named Natalie Portman.

But serving as an understudy was far from the extent of Britney's ambitions in New York. Carving out time from her schoolwork and the theater, she dragged Lynne around the city as she tried out for commercial after commercial – a handful of which she landed easily. She also appeared on Star Search in 1992, competing in the category of Junior Vocalist, a category that had been won the year before by LeAnn Rimes. Britney's talent was noteworthy on the show, but she ultimately lost to Blake McIver Ewing.

Later that year, right around the time of her eleventh birthday, Britney auditioned once more for the Mickey Mouse Club. This time, though, her age was no obstacle to her immediate acceptance into the cast.

The All-New Mickey Mouse Club – to differentiate it from the original show, which had run from 1955-1959, and The New Mickey Mouse Club, which was the 1977 revival – was a variety show, perfectly constructed to showcase the budding talents of Britney and her fellow Mouseketeers. The show was known for its sketch comedy, in which the kids took on different roles, occasionally improvising. For Britney, though, the main focus was the singing and dancing. She had already debuted on stage after stage; now, though, she had the chance to do what she loved on television, in front of an audience of thousands.

The Mickey Mouse Club was also packed with her peers – her true peers, kids her age who were both talented and driven, determined to make something of themselves through performing. Britney sang alongside Christina Aguilera and Justin Timberlake – whom she would later date for a time – and acted alongside a young Keri Russell and Ryan Gosling. In amongst the names that were destined to become famous, Britney is even now consistently included in lists of the most successful former Mouseketeers – which isn't surprising, considering that she's frequently been named one of the biggest entertainers in history.

Not bad for a junior Disney alumni.

# CHAPTER THREE

In 1994, Britney discovered that all good things must come to an end: The All-New Mickey Mouse Club was canceled, and the Mouseketeers dispersed back to their hometowns and normal, non-Disneyfied lives. For more than twenty years, Britney's version of the show was not only the most recent, it was the most definitive; even when the show was revived again in 2017 (it went from the Mickey Mouse Club, to the New Mickey Mouse Club, to the All-New Mickey Mouse Club, to simply Club Mickey Mouse, avoiding the perhaps too-obvious choice of Brand New Mickey Mouse Club, For Reals This Time), it lasted only a single season and had far less impact on the lives of the child performers involved.

Britney was nearly thirteen years old when the show ended, and returned to Kentwood armed with a headful of performance knowledge and an ambition that was nowhere near satisfied. She enrolled in Parklane Academy for school, located in nearby McComb, Mississippi. It was a private school, but seemed worlds apart from the Professional Performance Arts School in New York. With her usual determination, Britney set herself the task of making the most of "normal" life. "I had fun when I was younger," she recalled years later. "I was a pretty normal girl, a tomboy." She played with her younger sister, endured teasing from her brother, and spent long hours talking over her dreams with her aunt Sandra, who was like a second mother to her.

Britney disliked the cliquish nature of the kids in the private academy, and determinedly set out to make friends with whoever she wanted, regardless of whether they were a cheerleader or a burnout. Vivid memories of playing basketball for the school team, of attending prom with her boyfriend Reg, of hanging out with her mixed group of friends – including a boy her age named Jason Alexander – of returning to gymnastics classes, all illustrated a perfectly respectable, perfectly worthwhile normalcy for a girl in her early teens; but for a girl with Britney's drive, it was practically torturous.

"I was so bored," she would say of her early teens, not too many years after. "I wanted more."

She was determined not to give up, even with all the distractions that came from living as a teenager. School, friends, chores, hobbies – everything came second to her drive, and her parents continued to support her. They were long past attempting to talk their middle child into delaying her music career until she was older; she'd already proven that she could handle a taste of fame.

Early in 1997, at age fifteen, Britney attracted the attention of band manager Lou Pearlman. Pearlman was a former blimp manufacturer who had hit on the idea of standardizing – and monetizing – the boy band business model of New Kids on the Block. Using his record label, Trans Continental Records, he had already launched the Backstreet Boys and NSYNC – featuring Britney's old Mouseketeer partner, Justin Timberlake. With the formula for success in place, Pearlman was developing a number of other bands simultaneously. One of them was a prospective girl group called Innosense, and he wanted to bring Britney on board.

Britney was ecstatic over the idea of doing something – anything! – other than simply continuing to live her normal life. She'd had a few years now of school, friends, chores, hobbies, on repeat; still singing her heart out every chance she got, she was ready to leap at the chance to join the ranks of teen pop groups.

This time, it was Lynne who thought Britney could go a little further.

Armed with some photos of her daughter and a tape of Britney singing a karaoke version of a Whitney Houston number, Lynne turned to a friend of the family, entertainment lawyer Larry Rudolph. Rudolph had a law firm based in New York, but had already considered taking on talent management along with his main role. Impressed – as so many others had been – by Britney's voice and her talent for entertaining, Rudolph decided that he was ready to take Britney on as his first management client.

"Set the girl group on the back burner for now," he advised Lynne. "Britney's got what it takes to be a solo artist – she just needs a demo."

Given this suggestion, Britney was only too happy to agree. Innosense was penciled in, not inked – and she picked up the song that Rudolph sent to her, a Toni Braxton number, and threw herself into rehearsing. Rudolph was determined to get her in front of record executives as quickly as possible, before Pearlman took over Britney's future; with his pushing and set timeline, she had only a week to practice the new song before her appointment at the recording studio.

Britney's first time in a recording studio was something she never quite forgot, despite the plethora of times that followed it over the years to come. The soundproofing on the walls of the booth, the bank of electronics shiny with flashing lights, the heavy embrace of the headphones, the microphone – a far cry from singing into a hairbrush in the bathroom, from monopolizing the TV to harmonizing with Madonna's music videos, from waiting in the wings for her chance to take the stage off-Broadway.

She had come so far – and she still had so far to go.

At the end of the summer of 1997, Britney and Lynne returned from their trip to New York to meet with record executives and hand out the demo tape. Both were exhausted – and disappointed.

*Ms. Spears, I'm afraid we have to pass.* If Britney never heard that phrase again in her life, it would be too soon. Her father called up Lou Pearlman and signed Britney on for Innosense, but even that wasn't enough to perk up her spirits. Given a glimpse of what it would be like as a solo artist, she wasn't sure that she was willing to settle for being part of a girl group.

She tried to settle back into her normal life. School was approaching; she had her friends, she reminded herself. But her relationship with her boyfriend Reg had already become strained. He was changing, she felt, not her – it was almost as though her brush with success had made him start to doubt himself. "I was really head over heels in love," she would say, not long after their breakup. "I don't think I'll ever love somebody like that again."

It was the first time that Britney was faced with being treated differently because of her career – but, sadly, it was far from the last.

"Normal" life was hard enough for Britney, but with

her first breakup on the horizon, it was even more difficult. She drew closer to her family, feeling as though they were the only ones who would always be there for her – no matter what happened. Maybe her stalling career was a disappointment to her parents, but it didn't even matter, because it was a disappointment to her, too.

And then, an interminable two weeks after her trip to New York, the phone rang.

# CHAPTER FOUR

Britney's demo had made the rounds at Jive Records, but it was more than her voice that stuck in their minds.

Years later, Barry Weiss, the president of Jive Records, would recall being shown "a picture of this really pretty young woman on a red and white picnic blanket, almost like a tablecloth from one of those small, local Italian restaurants. It was kind of funny. I think she might have had a dog in the picture as well, almost like Dorothy from Kansas."

Britney's all-American, girl-next-door persona immediately set her apart from much of her competition; she wasn't trying to be anything that she wasn't. Still, when she appeared for her in-person audition with the executives of Jive Records, accompanied by Larry Rudolph, she dressed up to look a little older than her sixteen years, wearing a black cocktail dress and high heels. With coaching from Rudolph and her mother, she had chosen

Whitney Houston's *I Have Nothing* as her audition song.

Whitney Houston had been one of Britney's top three favorite artists from the time she was young, and it felt natural and right to pay respect and homage to Houston as she took this next big step in her own career. However far she came, Britney promised herself, she would never forget the idols that had helped her to dream big.

Standing in front of the executives after singing her heart out, Britney waited for the response – which wasn't long in coming—thunderous applause.

The then-senior vice president of A&R, Jeff Fenster, later recalled "It's very rare to hear someone that age who can deliver emotional content and commercial appeal." But Britney, belying her age, had delivered both in buckets – and more than that, her determination was obvious. "Clearly [she is] a self-motivating person from a very young age."

Songwriter and producer Max Martin remembered, "It was pretty obvious that she had something, even though she was very quiet and very shy."

Jive Records signed Britney on immediately, guaranteeing the sixteen-year-old eight studio albums. Looking forward, for Britney, the production and release of eight albums seemed like it would take forever, as though her contract would last through her entire life. And here she was, just at the very beginning.

Jive's first step in developing Britney into the solo artist sensation the executives believed she could be was to assign her to work with a producer, Eric Foster White. White became a mentor to Britney in her early days at the record label, helping her to assess her voice as it was and to push it, to mold it, to see what it could be. Britney had envisioned herself as making "adult contemporary" music, a sort of "[younger] Sheryl Crow." But White had other ideas. Boy bands and girl groups had turned pop on its ear, and glossy up-tempo tunes were all the rage. With his training and suggestions, Britney's lower, rougher vocals were quickly shaped into the distinctively smooth, shiny pop tone that would become her trademark. The songs she sang had to match. Her early ideas of the tone of her work were quick to fall by the wayside once she heard the results of White's coaching; "It made more sense to go pop," she would say later, reflecting on her early loves of not just music but also movement, "because I can dance to it — it's more me."

And Britney was determined to be herself, no matter what came next.

With the first sessions under White's coaching the benchmark to judge the next step, Jive executives sent Britney off to record her first studio album in Cheiron Studios, located in Stockholm, Sweden. Among the host of producers and developers who worked with her, songwriter and producer Max Martin was at the forefront. Martin was a middle-aged Swede with long hair – "I looked like Ozzy Osborne" – and had worked with artists and bands such as Ace of Base and the Backstreet Boys. He had a unique approach to glossy pop that Britney liked, and though the two were only slated to collaborate on two songs, they ended up recording eight in total for the first album.

Britney was willing to work hard and fast, and the recording sessions put her determination to the test. "I didn't know what to expect," she said, of both going to Sweden and recording her first album. "It was my first time overseas. They had six songs, I had a week. I never even saw Sweden, we were so busy!"

The sixteen-year-old's work ethic made an impression on Max Martin, too, who later remembered how their first session had gone. "We'd been going for eight hours. I could hear her stomach growl in the microphone. I asked if she was hungry. She said, "No, I'm fine." I said, "Let's take a break," and she had three burgers."

Martin was the writer behind what would become Britney's first single, ...Baby One More Time. Though the two were an odd couple, it was partly due to Britney's comfort level with Martin that she felt free to ad-lib when she first began to record the song – the opening of *Ooh, baby, baby* wasn't in the original lyrics. Barry Weiss later recalled, "We thought it was really weird at first. It was strange. It was not the way Max wrote it. But it worked!"

And *how*. Britney's ad-lib became something of a catchphrase for her throughout her career; it's almost difficult to look back on it and realize that it wasn't even intended to be in the song to begin with, let alone the fact that when the teenager threw it in during recording, the response in the booth was, "Well, *that's* weird."

Britney completed recording of her first album in late spring 1998, without ever getting to see much of Stockholm. She returned home to find herself thrown into a promotional tour for the unreleased album, with most of the stops being held at shopping malls. Never one to give anything less than her all, Britney embraced every appearance, whether small or large, firmly believing that better things were coming down the pike.

And she was right – in January 1999, Jive Records released her first album, *...Baby One More Time*, and her entire world turned upside down. Suddenly, she was the Princess of Pop.

# CHAPTER FIVE

"**O**kay, Britney, let's take a look at the storyboard..."

Blonde hair tied back in a messy ponytail, Britney looked like the epitome of a bored teenager. Not at all like America's newest pop sensation, reviewing the ideas for her first music video.

"Um..."

To her befuddlement, the prospective outline for the video for *...Baby One More Time* was an "animated Power Ranger-y thing," more like a cartoon than anything else. Britney was so surprised that she hardly knew what to say – other than to straight-up tell them the truth.

"This," she told them, "is...not right. If you want me to reach four-year-olds, then OK, okay, but if you want me to reach my age group..."

They definitely wanted her to reach her age group. After a few moments of thought, Britney drew on her own past to suggest an entirely new direction for the video.

"So I had this idea where we're in school and bored out of our minds, and we have Catholic uniforms on..."

It was her own idea to tie up the shirt to keep it from being too "boring and cheesy." Every piece of clothing in the entire shoot was purchased at K-Mart and cost less than seventeen dollars apiece; it was like a real-life throwback to Britney's days at the private academy. But as prosaic as it was for her, the tied-up shirt and short plaid skirt became a fashion statement that turned into a fashion trend that became a fashion debate; every female artist of the time suddenly seemed to consider themselves contractually obligated to release a video where they bared their midriff. Embroiled in an ongoing discussion over whether she should be promoting such "sex appeal" to other teen girls, Britney would practically roll her eyes. "I didn't do *anything*," she told Rolling Stone later. "All I did was tie up my shirt."

If *...Baby One More Time* had been less of a sensation, then the question of whether Britney's shirt was tied or tucked would have likely been moot. But the album was released to a thunderous reaction, debuting at Number One on the US Billboard

200 and certified as two-times platinum within a month. It sold over ten million copies worldwide in its first year, and went down in history as the biggest-selling album of all time by a teenaged artist. The single, too, had made enormous waves, turning out to be one of the hottest-selling singles ever. By any artist in any demographic. In 2000, it earned Britney her very first Grammy nomination.

If Britney's tied-up school uniform had ruffled a few feathers after her first album was released, the second album seemed determined to follow suit. *Oops! I Did It Again* released in May 2000, only seventeen months after Britney's first album. It, too, debuted at number one in the US; it quickly surpassed *...Baby One More Time*, breaking records for the highest debut sales by a solo artist, and earning a spot on the list of the best-selling albums of all time. It also topped an admittedly short list of famous songs with *Oops* in the title.

In *Rolling Stone's* review of the album, the "cheese" of the pop music was acknowledged, but beneath it, Rob Sheffield wrote, Britney's artistry shone through: "complex, fierce...a true child of rock and roll tradition."

After the album's release, Britney embarked on her second headlining tour; before the release of ...Baby One More Time, she had been an opening act for NSYNC, making this her third national tour in total. With each one, she was determined to take a step up. Though only eighteen, Britney was already a consummate performer, led by a natural tendency and learned skill. Her shows quickly became known as knock-outs, ecstatic, beat-driven three-hour sessions that left everyone in attendance exhausted – except, it seemed, Britney herself. Her unbreakable energy continued to see her through, and she greeted each new stop on the tour as though it was the very first.

From the shy, quiet girl who had originally auditioned for the executives at Jive Records, to the show-stopping singer who held thousands of hearts in her hand – it seemed an almost impossible combination to belong to a single young woman. But Britney had found the key early on. Performing, she said, was "a boost to my confidence. It's like an alter-ego-type thing. Something clicks and I go and turn into this different person." She paused to think about it. "I think it's kind of a gift to be able to do that."

Still, she admitted, "I don't want to go over the top. I want to have a place to grow."

Britney was no longer a minor, but she was still a youthful role model for other girls younger than her, and the outfits that she chose for her performances drew wary criticism. Far from the kerfuffle that had been started with her Catholic schoolgirl outfit at sixteen, her performance at the 2000 MTV Video Music Awards lit an outright fire as she appeared in a flesh-colored bodysuit; reviewers noted that she was already showing signs of becoming a more "provocative" performer – signs that would prove more and more accurate over the years. But from the start, Britney was quick to shrug off any deeper intention below her costume choices.

"Look, hand on the Bible – I know I'm not ugly, but I don't see myself as a sex symbol or this goddess-attractive-beautiful person at all. When I'm on stage, that's my time to do my thing—and it's fun. It's exhilarating just to be something that you're not. And people tend to believe it."

People believing it, for many critics, was at the heart of the issue. But Britney, though a trend-setter, was far from the only young female artist who chose to dress provocatively in her shows. It was part of performing, in her mind – another way to attract the attention of the people in the audience, or the folks listening to the radio, or the potential album buyers in the local Sam Goody or Tower Records. She had always believed in herself; the idea of a million plus others believing in her too was nice, but felt almost imaginary. Living at home in Kentwood with her parents and younger sister, she still prayed every day, though her tours had interfered with the regularity of her churchgoing. In the same year that she graduated from high school, she also bought a vacation home in Destin, Florida. Sometimes she was that all-American girl next door; sometimes she was the pop sensation with the albino python as part of her costume.

At all times, though, she was just Britney.

# CHAPTER SIX

In 1999, Britney reconnected with a former Mouseketeer who had also turned into a pop sensation – NSYNC's Justin Timberlake.

Avoiding the challenges of fame within their own hometowns, both of them had chosen to finish out their schooling via a distance learning program through the University of Nebraska High School. They graduated the same year. With similar lifestyles and some shared experiences – as well as the fact that Justin had crushed hard on Britney when they were Mouseketeers together – the two became friends – and it wasn't long before the press were speculating that they had become something more. In late 1999, Britney and Justin announced that the speculation was right; Britney had her second official boyfriend, with her first being the long-forgotten Reg back at Parklane Academy.

This relationship was markedly different. Not only was Britney not a fifteen-year-old, she was also dating in the public eye – the very public eye. Britney quickly became known as someone who wore her heart on her sleeve, never shying away from speaking out about how she felt. "We've gone through so much together and we've known each other since we were 12 years old," she told The Observer in 2001. "We know each other inside and out. It's a deeper love than it was when I was younger."

The pop power couple made some intriguing decisions throughout their time together – such as the iconic matching all-denim outfits they wore to the American Music Awards in 2001 – but it was their back and forth after their breakup that drew the most attention. Despite the years of friendship and two years of dating, when the split came, it hit them both hard, proving dramatically how difficult it can be to carry on a relationship under the intense scrutiny of the public.

2001 was a big year, in a string of big years, for Britney's career. Though she had only released two albums thus far and had only been performing for three years, she was given the honor of hosting the 28th Annual American Music Awards along with LL Cool J. Nominated for both Favorite Female Pop Artist and Artist of the Year, she performed *Stronger* from her second album.

Later in the year, she joined Aerosmith and NSYNC as a special guest on the Super Bowl halftime show.

In amongst all her appearances, she ducked into the studio to record her third album. She was determined to take a different approach with this one; while touring, she had been inspired by artists such as Jay Z and the Neptunes, and wanted to make the next album "nastier and funkier." The glossy bubblegum pop of the previous two albums needed a little adjusting; working on the songs, she took every opportunity to add a hip-hop twist. She wrote five of the twenty-three songs that she recorded for the album, and narrowed the track list down to twelve. It was the first album, she said, that she had really "taken [her] time on," the first that she had written for – and with just a taste of what that felt like, she knew it was something she wanted for herself moving forward.

At nearly twenty years old, Britney felt as though she were at something of a crossroads. The morphing, changing style of her musical tastes seemed symbolic of who she was as a person; she poured herself into the album, feeling closer and more attached to the message behind it than she had felt to anything she'd done before. "It's really where I'm at right now and something I can really relate to," she said of the album. When it came time to name it, it seemed only natural that it should be self-titled *Britney*.

The extra time and care she took with the album resonated with her audience and garnered her a whole new set of listeners. One reviewer recognized that the sound was "more adult while still recognizably Britney...the work of a star who has now found and refined her voice, resulting in her best record yet." *Britney* earned two more Grammy nominations for its namesake artist.

In 2002, Britney made Forbes' list of the most powerful celebrities. Out of a list of one hundred big names, only one was at the very top – Britney Spears.

# CHAPTER SEVEN

After co-writing some of the material for her third album and realizing how much closer it brought her to her music, Britney was determined to involve herself in every aspect of the creation of the songs she recorded. When it came time to return to the studio for her fourth album, In The Zone, she followed through on her promise to herself.

Co-writing the songs gave her more control of what she put out into the world; co-producing gave her more control of how it sounded. Her heart had been on her sleeve; now it was in her music, in the lyrics, in the sound.

"I don't know if I'm the best songwriter in the world," she told a reporter with a cheerful, humble grin. "But I'm having fun with it. I'm learning."

Her learning experience resulted in one of her best-received albums. *In The Zone* was listed on

National Public Radio's compilation of the Fifty Most Important Recordings of the Decade; more than one reviewer noted how well the album showcased Britney's development as a songwriter. It also resulted in handing Britney her first Grammy win after six previous nominations.

While Britney's career was continuing on the up and up, her music wasn't the only thing that landed her in the tabloids in 2004.

Early on a Saturday morning, Britney stood next to a grinning, obviously-nervous dark-haired young man at the Little White Wedding Chapel in Las Vegas. It was January 3rd, and absolutely frigid outside. Britney wore the same thing she had worn out when she'd been picked up the evening before to head out on the town – baggy jeans with tears in the legs, a baseball cap. The bemused limo driver from her hotel had walked her down the aisle. At her side was Jason Alexander, a Kentwood native, whom she'd known since they were in elementary school together.

Britney wasn't entirely sure how she'd ended up there. She liked Jason – maybe she loved him. At the moment, she did, anyhow. They'd known each other forever, and she knew he was a decent guy. Solid. Small-town, honest. Still, the wedding was nothing if not spur of the moment; a junior at Southeastern Louisiana University, he had taken advantage of the winter break to come to meet up with her in Vegas and they'd been hanging out and then one thing had led to another.

The story of the aftermath ranges depending on who is telling it. One thing is for certain – the wedding of Britney Spears and her childhood friend Jason Alexander lasted less than sixty hours before it was annulled. The story hit the newspapers and spread like wildfire; at the time, Britney's attorney, David Chesnoff, spoke on the matter, saying plainly, "There is no marriage now. [They both] agreed to this completely. They've made a wise decision. I know they care about each other. They are friends."

Though both of them were twenty-two years old, and the chapel owner stated definitely that neither were intoxicated, the annulment request stated that Britney had been "incapable of agreeing to the marriage" because she "lacked understanding of her actions."

In an interview at the time, Britney said, "It was me being silly, being rebellious." It was a joke that went too far, she told reporters – and her family agreed.

Years later, though, Jason Alexander would claim that neither he nor Britney had wanted the annulment, and that it was forced on them by her family. Some saw the incident as a warning sign of the control that Britney's family had over the young woman – but in all likelihood, it will be impossible to ever know the truth about what happened that crazy Saturday morning in Las Vegas.

What is undeniable is the fact that just seven months after the annulment, Britney married backup dancer Kevin Federline. This time, the marriage stuck for a little while longer than fifty-five hours.

In October 2004, the month after her wedding to Federline, Britney posted a "letter of truth" on her fan website.

"I'm going to take some time off to enjoy life," she wrote. She had been missing too many of the simple things – and she believed that her recent fall, causing damage to her knee, had "happened for a reason," to give her no choice other than step back for a while and allow her body a chance to rest up and recover. "It's amazing what advisors will push you to do, even if it means taking a naive young blonde girl and putting her on the cover of every magazine. My prerogative right now is to just chill and let all of the other overexposed blondes on the cover of Us Weekly be your entertainment. Good luck girls!"

At the same time, in the letter, she spoke of what she hoped would be her next big project in life: becoming a mother.

The idea of taking time off and becoming a mother would seem counterintuitive to almost anybody else; only someone with Britney's by-now-legendary inexhaustible energy and enthusiasm could possibly believe that the two are compatible.

Still, she poured herself into those goals with the same hundred-percent attention that she gave to everything else. Though her marriage to Federline was far from perfect – for one thing, it raised eyebrows because at the time of their wedding, he had only recently broken up with his previous girlfriend, who was pregnant with his second child – she was determined to give it her all. In April 2005, she and Federline announced that they were expecting their first child together.

Being pregnant, Britney told People Magazine, was "empowering – it brings out a pure side of you."

From the beginning, Britney embraced the thought of being a mother. She had been close with her own mother throughout her life. She knew that marriage was far from a cakewalk – her own parents, though they had stuck together throughout the time that their children were growing up, finally divorced in 2002, and after a stressful, dramatic childhood, Britney would say that it was the best thing that could have happened for them. But her mother had always believed that the children she'd borne were the saving grace of her complicated marriage, and Britney hoped that, if nothing else, she could have the same saving grace in her children.

Britney's first child, Sean Preston, was born in September 2005. Britney fell in love with him at first sight. She had been raised Baptist, had studied Kabbalah with her friend Madonna, but with Sean

Preston in her life, she announced, "My baby is my religion." Everything good in the world seemed to be caught up in the little bundle – which only made it more confounding when, in early 2006, Britney was photographed by the press driving a car with Sean Preston in her lap, rather than a car seat.

The fallout was horrific. The idea that a loving mother would jeopardize the safety of her infant, not yet six months old, caused a media frenzy and a strong backlash against Britney. Britney, for her part, understood the reaction – she publicly acknowledged her mistake, trying to explain the reasons that had led up to it. She'd spent years hounded by the paparazzi; it was bad enough to deal with them for her own sake, but with the added worry of her baby, she had made a bad decision as she tried to get away from photographers. The fact that the paparazzi itself had caught images of this bad decision lent credence to Britney's story; still, the public was divided on how to respond. In theory, an outcry about endangerment from unethical publicity hounds should raise compassion and understanding; after all, there have been multiple incidents in which a publicity-feeding frenzy has led to danger and even to death, such as in the case of Princess Diana. Largely, the continued skepticism of Britney's story was due in part to how she delivered the explanation, and in part, to other questionable decisions she had made in the past: the annulment of the previous year and the phrases "incapable" and "lacked understanding of her actions" came back to haunt Britney.

Regardless of exactly how things had happened, it was undeniable that the attention of the press had put a great deal of pressure on Britney – and after dealing with it for several years, it was no surprise that it might lead her to make poor decisions.

In 2006, Britney gave birth to her second child, Jayden James. He was born almost exactly a year after his older brother. Britney treasured her new boy as much as she cherished her first; however, the stresses that had been on her marriage from the very beginning had taken their toll, and two months after Jayden's birth, she filed for divorce from Federline, citing irreconcilable differences.

As much of a blessing as Britney's two boys were to her, some hard changes were just around the corner.

# CHAPTER EIGHT

Towards the end of 2006, as Britney tried to get herself settled as a single mother, she was faced with a deeply unpleasant reality: the looming sensation of impending loss.

Britney's home life had always been more than a little chaotic. Though her parents had given her the attention she so craved, she'd always known that their marriage was strained. When things had been at their worst, she'd turned to her mother's sister, Sandra Covington, for comfort. Aunt Sandra had been like a second mother to Britney; as loving as Lynne was, Britney had adored her Aunt Sandra and made her a confidant throughout her childhood.

Now, she was dying.

Sandra had been diagnosed with ovarian cancer in 2002, and Britney had joined her mother in doing everything she could to help care for her beloved aunt. The fight had been long and hard;

"I pray every night about it," Britney told People Magazine. Seeing how the struggle had impacted her mother, especially in the year of Lynne and Jamie's divorce, had struck Britney deeply. And now, with Sandra slipping away a little more with every day, in the year of Britney's own divorce, the shock of confronting loss slammed down on her like a closing door.

In January 2007, Sandra Covington succumbed to her cancer. Grieving the loss but unable to cope with facing it head-on, the next several months saw a series of bizarre and questionable decisions from Britney. In February, she checked herself into a drug rehabilitation facility in Antigua; however, that refuge lasted for less than a day. Restless, she checked herself back out again and returned to the United States immediately. The next night, paparazzi looking on, she took a pair of electric clippers from the hairdresser at a salon in Los Angeles and slowly, deliberately shaved her own head.

"My mom," she said with a half-grin, staring at herself in the mirror, "is going to freak."

Britney's inability to deal with the grief of losing her aunt could not have come at a more inopportune time. Initially, she and Kevin Federline had agreed on sharing custody of their two boys; however, in light of her bizarre actions and the fact that she was checking herself in and out of treatment facilities, her share of the custody was suddenly dubious. In the midst of all of that, her actions also led to an estrangement from her mother, Lynne, who was dealing with her own overwhelming grief over losing her sister. By October 2007, Britney had lost custody of Sean Preston and Jayden James; Federline had the boys, and she had only visitation rights. The reasons for the change of custody were not officially revealed to the public; however, it was open to speculation, and given her recent erratic behavior, it wasn't a surprise to anyone – except perhaps Britney herself.

Numb from the chaos and tragedy of the year, Britney poured her attention into the recording studio, seeking a reprieve from the trauma of her everyday life. The result was her fifth studio album, *Blackout* – released the same month that she lost custody of her boys. After a record-setting four number-one debuts, *Blackout* was the first not to join its predecessors, possibly in part due to the backlash from her very public behavior. Still, the album received positive reviews and was awarded Album of the Year at the MTV Europe Music Awards, among other recognitions. Britney's star had not stalled – even though her personal life was in a plummet.

Distraught at the thought of losing her sons, she refused to hand over custody when it was time. The refusal ended up with Britney being placed in a psychiatric ward under a 5150 – an involuntary psychiatric hold. While in the ward, she was stripped of her visitation rights for the boys, and Federline was granted complete legal and physical custody.

Years later, looking back at that devastating time, Britney would say, "I was lost... I didn't know what to do with myself. I was trying to please everyone around me because that's who I am deep inside. There are moments where I look back and think: 'What the hell was I thinking?'" Her history of fame from an early age deserved a piece of the responsibility, she agreed. "Each and every one of us that starts at a young age needs to take into account that you've got to be balanced in order to stay in this industry and manage your personal life... Sometimes that's very challenging. I think I was very different back then, not always knowing what's good or bad. Very instinctive."

After five days in the psychiatric ward at Ronald Reagan UCLA Medical Center, Britney was placed under a conservatorship led by her father and an attorney, Andrew Wallet. They had complete control of her assets, of her career, of what she did – of her life.

She was free of the ward – but she had stepped out into an entirely different type of enclosure.

# CHAPTER NINE

Doing her best to escape the aftermath of the trainwreck year that was 2007, Britney put her attention back into her career. A series of ventures, new and old, followed: guest starring on TV shows, winning awards, performing, filming videos, recording music, and contributing to a documentary about herself called Britney Spears: For The Record, which followed her return to recording after her break. In 2008, she released her next album, Circus, which returned to form by debuting at number one. Her music career was kicking back into high gear.

More importantly, after what seemed like far too long a stretch, she regained her visitation rights with her sons. She still carried grief – and scars – from the trauma of the previous year, but feeling her boys' arms around her in a loving hug helped her to heal more than anything else had.

"I'm at a better place in my life," she told an

interviewer. "My kids shaped my personality and filled me. They made me not worry about what was happening to me... My boys don't care if everything isn't perfect, they don't judge me. The best relationship I've ever had is with my boys."

In 2012, Britney joined the judges on X Factor for two seasons. She mentored the Teens category. When Britney was a teen herself, only seventeen, she had told a reporter, "You want to be a good example for kids out there and not do something stupid... if [kids] find something that keeps them happy — writing, drawing, anything like that — then they'll have confidence." Singing was the thing that brought Britney confidence and happiness, and she was eager to share that with others. After two years, though, the teens had taught Britney as much as she had taught them, it seemed – "Watching them all do their thing up on that stage every week made me miss performing so much! I had an incredible time doing the show, and I am so proud of my teens, but it's time for me to get back in the studio. I can't wait to get back out there and do what I love most."

In late 2012, around the time of her thirty-first birthday, Britney started to record her eighth album, Britney Jean. It was her final album under her original contract, signed back in 1997 – fifteen years and what seemed like several lifetime's worth of notoriety had come and gone. She had been so young then – it seemed impossible that she was still a young woman now, after everything she'd been through.

Two marriages, one annulment, one divorce. Two children. An ongoing residency in Las Vegas. Eight albums.

And all in only fifteen years.

# CHAPTER TEN

For the next few years, Britney's life settled into a more even keel. It was far from staid, normal, and boring: she wrote, recorded, acted, released albums, performed, and most importantly, spent time with her kids. Still, it was a time of relative normalcy that felt like a breath of fresh air after the tumult of her late twenties.

In 2019, though, the stress was back on – and harder than ever.

It started when her father, Jamie suffered a rupture of the colon – a medical emergency that was nearly fatal. Jamie and Lynne had reconciled a few years prior, though they had not remarried. Britney's relationship with both her mother and her father had gone through notable ups and downs; still, the stress over her father's condition seemed to lead to the cancellation of her residency in Las Vegas and her readmittance to a psychiatric ward. The next month, a source came forward, claiming to be part of the Spears legal team – the residency cancellation was a retaliation from Jamie Spears against Britney for "not taking her medication," and Britney's admittance to the psychiatric facility was involuntary; according to the source, she was being held there against her will, without reason other than her father's say-so as her conservator. The source also claimed that the conservatorship, which had been instated in 2008 with Britney's first admittance to a psychiatric ward, was supposed to have terminated the following year, in 2009.

Britney herself did not speak directly on the subject, but her silence only added to the furor. Outraged on her behalf – without knowing what the exact truth of the matter was – fans began to use #FreeBritney to protest her being held in the ward and demand her freedom. The movement gained traction quickly, with supporters like Paris Hilton, Cher, Miley Cyrus, and even the American Civil Liberties Union all throwing their weight behind it. A few months later, a judge ruled that there should be an evaluation of the conservatorship; Jamie was temporarily replaced as conservator, but later stated that the movement was nothing but a "conspiracy theory" and a "joke."

A lot of back and forth with the conservatorship followed over the next few agonizing years. It wasn't until 2021, when Britney was allowed to speak for herself on the matter before the court, that it was revealed that she had pushed for the end of the conservatorship for years. It had been "abusive," she said, keeping her from doing what she wanted with her life – even something as fundamental as getting married again and having another child. Without the permission of her conservator, she couldn't even make a doctor's appointment to remove her IUD. She had been put on lithium against her will, and when she told her parents that the medication made her nervous, a team of nurses came to observe her in her home. The conservatorship had granted her father power over her finances, restricting her use of credit cards; it had even kept tight control over smaller things such as changes in her house, like re-staining her kitchen cabinets.

"The last time I spoke [in court]," Britney told the judge, "made me feel like I was dead, like I didn't matter, like nothing had been done to me, like you thought I was lying. I want to be heard. I'm telling you this again so that maybe you understand the depth and degree of the damage...I want and deserve changes going forward. I don't owe anybody anything. I just want my life back."

As she spoke to the court, Britney broke down in tears, filled with overwhelming anger and sadness. As always, she wore her heart on her sleeve.

In November 2021, the judge finally put an end to Britney's conservatorship. For the first time since 2008, she was finally a free woman – and she knew that it was due in a large part to the push from her fans.

"You have no idea what it means to me to be supported by such awesome fans!" she wrote. "God bless you all!"

For the first time in a long time – maybe the first time ever – Britney had the freedom to choose – and the freedom to use her voice.

# CHAPTER ELEVEN

In June 2022, a small crowd of guests gathered for the intimate wedding ceremony outside of Britney's Thousand Oaks home in Los Angeles, California. The occasion was beautiful – and more than a little chaotic.

Before the ceremony itself, police were called to arrest an intruder: Jason Alexander, Britney's childhood friend and husband of less than three days, had stewed over his aborted marriage to the star for too long. Attempting to crash the wedding, he broke into her home armed with a knife. Though it's uncertain what his plan was, the outcome was clear whether he intended it or not: utter chaos.

Despite the chaos, Britney married her longtime boyfriend, Sam Asghari. The two had met and started dating in 2016; he was a model and fitness instructor who had appeared alongside Britney in the video for *Slumber Party*. Now that she was free to make her own decisions without needing the permission and endorsement of a conservator, she was eager to get started with the next part of her life: marriage and another child.

The marriage to Asghari, however, lasted a much shorter time than their dating had. By August 2023, they had split up, though Britney's desire to find love and have more children had not faded. She had loved being pregnant, loved becoming a mother, loved the "pure" side that it brought out in her. It made her feel most truly herself, and her sons were the loves of her life.

Despite the trauma she had been through, Britney continued to be an optimist about her personal relationships. This one and that one had not worked out – but there was always the next, just waiting around the corner.

Bad dates and breakups happened to everyone, she told a reporter. "Being famous doesn't make you any different."

With the chaos of her third wedding, the #FreeBritney movement leading to the end of her conservatorship, and the release of a duet with Elton John – *Hold Me Closer*, a remix of John's Tiny Dancer and Britney's first musical release since the termination of the conservatorship – the public interest in Britney's private life hit a resurgence. But though Britney had always been open about her life, as a chronically honest person with only a thin filter, she knew that enough was enough – for now, at least.

In a message to her fans, she reassured them that she was doing okay and asked that they respect her privacy.

With her current relationship at an end, Britney went back to what was most important to her: her sons. After the truth about her conservatorship had finally come to light, her relationship with her family continued to be strained. But her two sons were always there for her, her saving grace. And perhaps someday, around the corner, there would be more. She could always hope – and look to the future.

In July 2023, Britney announced that she would be releasing a memoir, telling her story in full for the first time, speaking up for herself. In addressing the court about the conservatorship, she had spoken of her desire to be heard. While under the conservatorship, her public statements had been dictated for her, her legal team advising her that she couldn't speak on the subject. Now that it was over, she wanted to tell everyone what had really happened. "I'd like to be able to share my story with the world. I have the right to use my voice."

Her own voice – not just lifted in song, but speaking on her own behalf.

Her own story – not told in a payback song by one of her exes, not spun by her conservator, not speculated on by the public.

Her own words. One hundred percent true. One hundred percent Britney.

Heart on her sleeve. Always.

Made in the USA
Las Vegas, NV
21 October 2023